MW01537894

Journals

(Music Edition)

Matthew Harper

Made in the USA
Las Vegas, NV
11 December 2023

82534647R10059